A TIME TO SING!

by

SID GOVE

Jetty House
an imprint of Peter E. Randall Publisher
Portsmouth, New Hampshire
2013

ISBN: 978-1-937721-13-8
Library of Congress Control Number: 2013948932

Jetty House
Portsmouth, NH
www.perpublisher.com

Book design: Grace Peirce

Other Publications by Sid Gove:
From Me to You! (2008) Vantage Press
'Til We Meet Again! (2011) Vantage Press

Dedicated to my grand-nephew
Mason Catuncan Gove

Contents

.

Preface

THIS TIME the reader will still meet picture-words, descriptive sentences and new ideas; as "twice" before. But, herein, the format may seem a little more serious, thoughtful and different in its initial greeting, plot and sound. (It was <u>so</u> planned!)

You'll still find new short-story poems and new idea patterns. But, there is also a newly added element that I have never before written about.

The last half includes an essay/short-story series noting "A Visitation," "A Near Death Surprise," and five sighted-visions. Since these are all personal events, I believe they deserve a rightful spot! Think of them as being a part of a "real" lifelong human adventure!

S. B. G.

Acknowledgments

Anyone, looking to buy "a copy" of the 1922 *Gove Book,* should turn to page 65.

Anyone, wishing to contact Gove, Kansas should check page 65.

A special thank you is extended to Ms. Mary LaMacchia, for typing my hand-printed manuscript.

Ms. Grace Peirce, who did the book's colored-cover design, additionally, helped to bring *A Time to Sing!* to a successful finish. <u>Most welcomed!</u>

Part I:

Spontaneous Reactions

_____

_____

_____

_____

_____

_____

_____

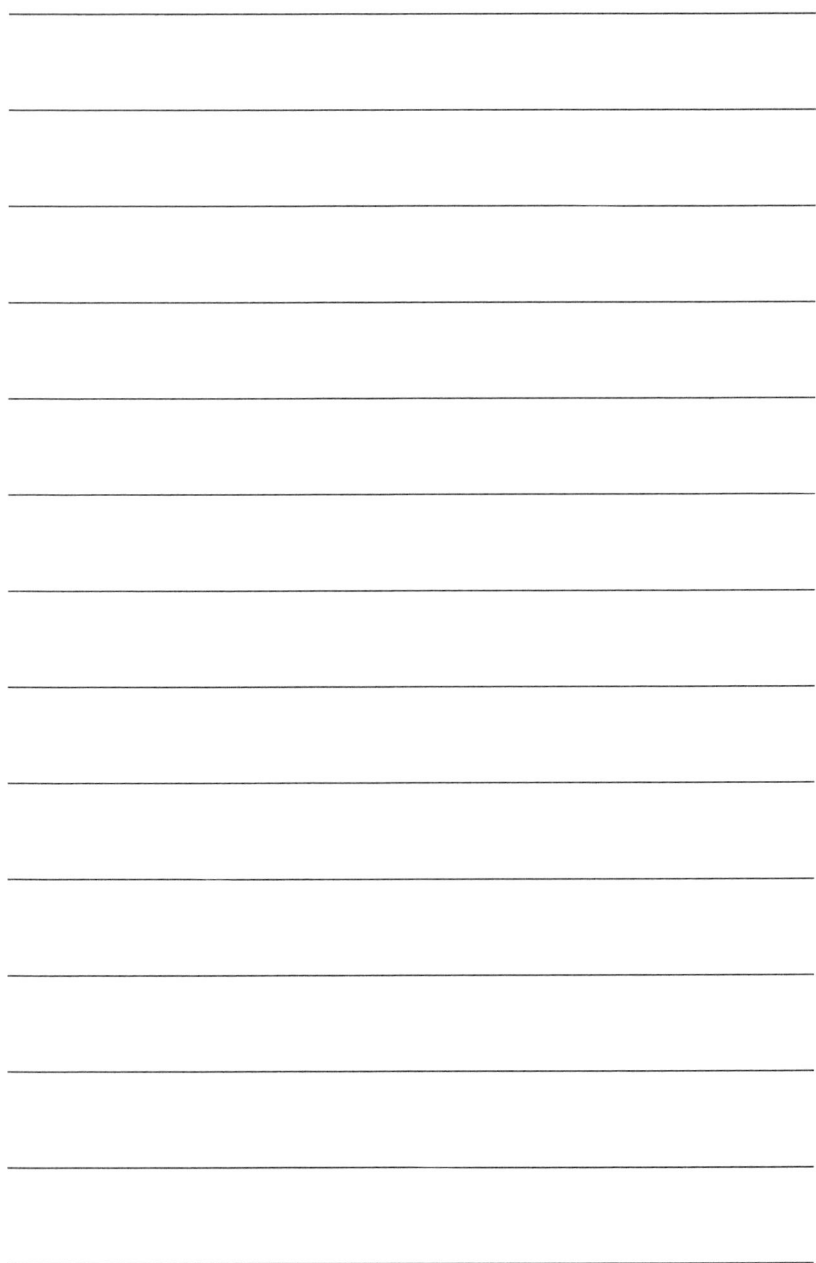

Who? . . . Is That Talking!

Who? . . . Is That Talking!
It's a rabbit, calling a hare.

Who? . . . Is That Talking!
It's the turbulent-winds
moving, whenever, they
dare.

Who? . . . Is That Talking!
It's the fall leaves,
before they color, drop
and dry.

Who? . . . Is That Talking!
It's only a very happy
"unseen" apple, on a
fruit tree; watching
humans quickly passing by.

Who? . . . Is That Talking!
It's the September
kids, starting "another"
adventurous school year.

Who? . . . Is That Talking!
It's retired teachers,
Having an afternoon
"tea break."

Who? . . . Is That Talking!
It's a race-track crowd,
Deciding on which horse
"to bet."

Who? . . . Is That Talking!
It's a nervous bank
manager, with no
more money, to let.

Who? . . . Is That Talking!
It's the vacationers,
worried about "the
goods" they are being
expected to buy.

Who? . . . Is That Talking!
It's the Holiday Spirits,
that continue to thrive,
because they don't tease,
as they once did, when
they were alive.

Alliterations

1. many mice, munching
   morning-morsels,
   mumbled mournfully

2. artists asked authors
   about ancient antiques

3. two teachers, tasting
   "tantalizing teas"

4. seven selected sailors,
   seen saluting, "smartly"
   Stateside

5. brown bottles bobbing
   brightly beside
   Benny Beaver's busy
   brook

6. fast-foods favor frantic
   families, from famine

7. police presence provides
   "peace," people proudly
   promote

8. cheerful children,
   counting chocolate
   covered candy coins

9. poor politics "pollute"
   plenty populations,
   profoundly

10. attentive audience,
    ate apples, afterwards

11. tall tales "tickle" the
    tonsils, totally

12. coloring crayons, commonly
    clustered, collected cobwebs

13. shifting sea sands,
    sparkled shells, simply

14. twelve teachers, travel
    turnpikes to think

15. when was washing
    windows, wasteful
    work

16. train tracks, "truly,"
    tie towns together

17. winter-winds whistled
    wildly, while Whitney,
    waited wistfully wringing wet

18. five fingers, fed five
    fussy fish, finally

19. dual-doorknobs, don't
    demand, double dusting

20. shy-students, sometimes
    "smile" singing simple
    songs

21. bullies believe, "Bombshell
    Blunders"

22. curious cats, catch
    creepy, crawling creatures

23. singing song sparrows,
    sat "silently" still

24. rapid road-repairs,
    really "rallied" rural
    residences

25. polo players probably, "plotted"
    point-potentials

26. salt-ships seen
    sailing southern
    seas, smoothly

27. stranded soldiers,
    sang salty-songs,
    some silly,
    some sad

28. Santa sings some
    stirring songs,
    seen shooting skyward,
    star-struck

29. tiny-tots, "tickled,"
    touching Tinker Toys

30. Will, whistles, when-
    ever working with wildlife-western
    wallpaper

31. global generosity,
    generally grows,
    given good-guidance

32. pink-picky piglets,
    playing politely, . . .
    pleased parents

33. teaching, teacher-
    tasks, through "time-
    tested" techniques

34. speakers "sounding-
    silly," silenced senior
    support, suddenly

35. tennis teams, trying
    to tackle, tough turfs

36. fewer fish, find
    fisherman, fearing
    financial failure

37. tasteful-tarts, tingle
    troubled tonsils

38. green gums, give guests,
    gentle giggles

39. who would "wonder,"
    when Wonder Woman
    WON

40. tell "Tip," to take "Toots,"
    travelling tonight

Bugs

Some, like to fly.
Some, like to crawl.

Some, like to dance,
Some, like to stall.

Some, like to visit.
Some, like to read.

Some, like to just sit.
Some, like the ocean-breeze.

Some, like my jam crackers.
Some, like to sneeze.

Some, like to bite.
Some, like to travel, at night.

Some, like to watch TV.
Some, like to see you and me.

New Hampshire Winters

The mid-winter snows,
like to tickle my nose.
And, to dry-out my lips
and my hair!

It's that time of the year,
when sled-runners
go snapping, cracking, and
popping, in the brisk,
sharp, icy New Hampshire
air!

With my Double-Dog skis,
I can travel, with the
greatest of ease…
over the hillsides
and through groves of
different tall trees,

I seldom, hit a bad rut,
or run out of my share
of good luck.
Although, I do so "with
care."

By not taking sudden turns
or sharp cuts, to upset
my new hat or my newly
cut hair!

Short-Takes

These pesty black flies,
are back!
They're biting my arms
and my neck.
They are also getting
into my eyes and ears.
We'll need a major
cold snap,
to clean out the air,
Everywhere!
Have no fear! Let's
hope, that "special time"
is very near!

Baby "chicks" are cute.
Baby "ducks" are, too.
Baby "turtles" are my
favorite.
Which, Baby, would
you most likely choose?

I see a jet,
up in the sky.
It's going by, so fast!
I wonder, why?
Do you suppose it'll have
enough fuel to last?

Oh! (pause) It is muggy!
Oh! (pause) It is hot!
Oh! (pause) It is drippy!
Oh! (pause) Where? Oh!
Where is there a dry spot?

What is that ant doing?
When did it "first" appear?
Where is it going?
Why is it in such a hurry?
No wonder!
It smells food, somewhere!

It's snowing? (Sort of!)
It's snowing! (Not much)
It's hard to believe!
It's visiting us, so late!
It's still, way out-of-touch!!

After several weeks of a long dry
spell, Mother Nature came knocking
on our door. Leaving us, with a bucket
filled with three inches of "raindrops,"
and not a dabit more. She left us,
with a promise, that she would soon
return. To wet down our dying
hay fields, lawns and food
crops, before they'd all
dried up or burned!

Relationships

Do fishermen really
like to sing?
One thing's for sure,
"wasps" like to sting!!

The school bands are
playing a catchy beat.
The beach crowd, are
trying "to escape" the
heat.

The political speakers,
have lost their notes.
Some nearby kids, have
turned them into spit-
balls. And that's no
joke!

Loud noises are hard on
one's ears.
Soft musical tunes can
bring about tears.

Can old tin cans really
talk?
Do dark clouds always
bring raindrops?

Birds, each day, cross
"freely" above many lands.
Small fishy sea creatures

seek safe shelters, like
tunnel rocks, shipwrecks
or open beer cans.

Summer suns bring about
clear blue skies.
Holiday "store sales," offer
shoppers attractive buys!

Run-away forest fires
make people very scared!
Unpaid tax bills, make
"tax collectors" very mad!

Why is it, at night, the stars are
always bright? While, in the day-
time, those same stars, are
out-of-sight?

Hot summer temperatures
dry-up the lawn grasses.
Long car and truck lines,
make it hard for vehicular
passes.

It's going to be another
hot day!
Plenty of drinks and
rest, will rule the
amount of work and play.

Who is missing? . . .
Half the bus!
Who are those?
Well! . . .
They don't belong "to us!"

When roads need a quick-
fix.
And, old shoes, need to be
dumped or ditched.

Dark-storm clouds are
forming in the heavenly skies . . .
Sand storms, can hurt
our delicate eyes.

Smile! Says, the blinking
billboard.
"Run!" says, the gathering
crowd.
"That picture, is from outer
space,
I surely, do allow!"

The work days are
getting "shorter."
But, the classroom
studies, are getting
"longer!"

Little Firefly

Little Firefly, Little Firefly!
Where have you been?

Little Firefly, Little Firefly!
Have you been out,
for a midsummer's nightly-
spin?

Little Firefly, Little Firefly!
Why aren't there more
of you?

Little Firefly, Little Firefly!
Where have you been, too?

Little Firefly, Little Firefly!
Seen, circling-around,
our sickly, stately old Ash-
Tree!

Little Firefly, Little Firefly!
Flashing your special light,
well into the darkness of
the night.

Little Firefly, Little Firefly!
Just like passenger planes
and cargo jets,
travelling the skies,
to everyone's delight.

Little Firefly, Little Firefly!
You aren't very much,
for looks.
But, you can sure do the
"Bubble Dance,"
while, in the countryside,
at the city parks
or the nearby riverside-
brooks!

Goals, I Try to Meet . . .

1. Easy, To Read
2. Easy, To Picture
3. Easy, To Understand
4. Easy, To Please

Can You…?

Can you fly?
Can you fly?
Like a bluebird,
up in the sky!

Can you walk?
Can you walk?
Like to stroll,
around a city-block!

Can you read?
Can you read?
Like to children,
home alone. Or,
whenever, there's
a need!

Can you swim?
Can you swim?
Like a toy fish,
on a flat dish!

Can you swing?
Can you swing?
Like touching the
sky,
as you speed or
as you wish!

Can you see?
Can you see?
Like, what the
future holds
for you and me?

Can you count?
Can you count?
Like figuring the
success rate,
that political parties
will try to mount!

Multiple Meanings

The sales clerk,
helped change
a ten dollar bill,
at a county fair.
Yes, indeed! Yes, indeed! (Thanks)

A local police officer,
stopped the traffic,
so a visitor could
cross the street.
Yes, Indeed! Yes, Indeed! (Welcome)

The elementary teacher,
told the class of thirty,
how "helpful"
they had been.
Yes, Indeed! Yes, Indeed! (Appreciated)

The city mayor,
introduced the guest speaker,
from the crime fighter's unit.
Yes, Indeed! Yes, Indeed! (Attention)

A hungry black bear
is scratching the ground,
while looking for food.
Yes, Indeed! Yes, Indeed! (Desperate)

The veterinary staff,
focused their skills
and attention toward
helping a very sickly lion.
But, to no avail!
Yes, Indeed! Yes, Indeed! (Despair)

A newly "approved" rejuvenation
drug, was carefully sprayed
into the patient's blinding-eyesight.
It worked!
Yes, Indeed! Yes, Indeed! (Rejoiced)

The Northern Lights,
Put on a dazzling nightly
display, over northern Canada.
Yes, Indeed! Yes, Indeed! (Impressive)

The summer-musical program,
brought together,
many talented people
of all ages, from near
and far.
Yes, Indeed! Yes, Indeed! (Recall)

Nose Drips, Revisited
(03-01-2012)

I'm really very sorry,
to regretfully report,
I'm under-the-weather,
with a very drippy nose.
So, I'm going to be very late,
today, for work!

It's kinda like having
a bad thunderstorm,
stuck "inside" my head.
It doesn't let me sleep
much, whenever I am in
my bed.

It always seems worse,
though,
when I'm up walking about.
Because, it makes me feel all
stuffed-up, dragging and
nearly all washed-out.

My mum tells me,
to drink lots of plain old water
and with glasses of healthy
orange juice.

And, to be sure, to get off to
bed real-early,
as it's bound, to do, some good!

But, you know, . . .
even these suggestions,
don't seem to help, very much.
When I have a throbbing
head-cold,
That wants to dance about,
a lot.

Father tries to be helpful.
He says, all I need is a
few spoonfuls of good
Old Father John's cough-syrup.
That's bound to do "the trick!"

Well, I suppose, it's possible.
But! Gosh! No, thanks, Dad!
Because, when I tried that the
last-time,
it only made me feel more sick!

Our family doctor,
has been called,
to check my cold and
to investigate "the germ."

"Here you go, there, son!
He says, to me.
"Try one of these.
Remember!
They'll work far better,
if you swallow each pill, whole.

Because they are time-
released capsules,
made to break-up a very bad cold."

The pills, he wants me to swallow,
are the same size as
Canada Mints.
But, seeing my fear and concern,
he has an "action plan,"
standing-by,
to immediately commence!

"Press-your-nose.
Close-both-eyes.
Pop-the-pill.
With-some-juice.
Let-it-slide.
Oh! How, wise!"
(unknown)

That night, I dreamt,
I was riding a
magnificent black and
white steed.
Holding a very sharp-sword,
in one hand,
and a well-made
protective shield,
with the other.

I'm now on my way,
to slay, a very pesky-dragon,
that likes to roar and dance!
He also, liked to eat plum
puddings, whenever, he's
given a chance!

This dragon has established
a very formidable beach-
head, that appears to be
very well hidden, protected
and safe.

But, to a determined-hunter,
who knows "what" he likes to eat.
This dragon, has already, lost
"the race!"

At King Arthur's Round Table,
accompanied by his fearless
and most trustworthy knights.
I was warmly treated, to a
bowl full of chocolate ice cream
and a hot plate of freshly-cooked
vegetables, meats and mixed
potato-rice!

An honor, that brought with it,
both instant fame and
personal delight,
on that joyous (no more
dragon) night!

Sometime, the very next
morning, when the sun
was up and beaming so bright
and clear
My "cold-drips" had departed
in the depleting mist
and foggy spring-time air.

As I looked outside my
upstairs bedroom window,
I was hit, by a most
astonishing sight!

There, lying upon our
just-cut front lawn,
was a dragon's tooth, that
had been carefully placed
(on the edge) sometime
during the predawn,
while there was "a mist"
and it was still, at night!

The Horseshoe Arc

On any clear sunny,
warm spring or
fall day, the all-boys
high school gym class
usually ventured,
to "The Great Outdoors,"
to help wake up
any early morning students
and to take full advantage
of the perfect weather!

It was, on one such
fateful occurrence,
when I was a sophomore
that my class was "introduced,"
to the game of . . .
Horseshoes!

The goal, was to touch
or circle the metal stake,
that loomed some distance,
up ahead.

Simple?
Sure!
No problem!
It was strongly emphasized.

It helped, to have good eye and good
hand coordination, however.
It also required, that the metal object thrown
be given enough forward thrust,
so the horseshoe would be able
to reach its designated target.

Trying, to reach any "new" physical
distance for the first time,
always made me uneasy.

But,
for some unknown reason,
no one, this time,
seemed to consider that
playing horseshoes could be . . .
      1.   A challenge!
      2.   A problem!
      3.   A disaster!

It was now "my turn"
to score, a deciding winning point!
Since, I was not allowed
to wear my daily glasses in PE,
it was always a troublesome
situation.

Well! With a strong, wildly
upward sweep and
with a quick release
that old horseshoe,
was sent on its way, home!

Just before, it reached
its highest mid-flight path,
I sensed a serious problem.
It was not headed in the
right direction!
Instead, it was barreling
(at high speed),
toward a nearby classmate.

There was no time, to say
any words.
So, I just let out a loud holler
and pointed to the horseshoe.

Strange! But, that old horseshoe,
seemingly-hovered for several seconds,
in one spot.
Thus, allowing everyone to look
and to move out of the way, safely!

However, the horseshoe, still landed
"only inches," in front of one of the
players, on the opposite team.
Oh! What a fuss that started!

"You tried to kill us!"
"Why did you do that?"
The questions seemed to roll on,
in a series of unrelenting whispering
waves.

I was speechless and shaken.
But, thankfully, no one was hit
or hurt.
And, no blood splattered about, either.
Apologies, followed!

Aftermath:
There were no more
Horseshoe Games,
for the rest of that season!

Part II:

Thoughtful Encounters

_____

_____

_____

_____

_____

_____

_____

A Tangible Visitation
(1960s)

Late, one evening, when I
was much younger, a Messenger
visited my upstairs bedroom.

Suddenly, unexpectedly, I sensed that
I was no longer, alone.

Someone (very quietly) was
standing on the right-hand side
of my bed, while I was on my back.

He touched me lightly (my eyes
remained closed), with His left
clinched fist, resting on my
left shoulder.

Then, so very carefully, the
clinched fist "slowly" opened,
to reveal a long, narrow, firm
feeling hand much longer than
my own.

Also, it needs to be noted, that
He had a thumb and four fingers,
just like all earthly humans.
(but in this case, no rings and no
wristwatch, detected.)

He then, proceeded "to tighten"
His grip. Until, I wondered,

at what point, this would likely
continue? I was just
about ready, to shout out loud, to
"Please stop!"

Just as unexpectedly (as if He had
been reading my mind), the hand
pressure came to a quick halt!

Then, through an ever-so-slow
progression forward, but in a
highly orchestrated movement,
He started to lessen His grip.

Perhaps, to show, that "the
purpose" has been finished.
Perhaps, to show me, that
the intended goal had been
fully met!
Perhaps, to show, that the
reason had been adequately
timed and was completed!

This Visiting-Appointee, then
started to glide away, from
the bed and from me.

Still, it was possible to follow
the direction and forward drift,
He had taken.

There were, no thought waves.
There was, no verbal communication.
There were, no lights.
There was, no change in the smells or feeling
of the bedroom air.

This Person-of-Mystery, did not
use the "nearest" exit, when He
decided to leave. But, instead,
the furthest spot in the room.
One, that would point to the
southwestern section, of the bedroom,
some extra walking/gliding distance
away.

This Lone-Spirit, continued His
forward movement slowly, carefully,
effortlessly across the room toward
the solid southwestern wall, which
lead to nothing more than "open
space," on the other side.

Strange, looking back, there wasn't
any thump, pop, scrape, or shake of
the wood lined-papered wall. Nor,
were there any "telltale" signs
or any marks left behind, from
"His passage," when the area was
later checked, the next morning.

Soon, thereafter (the very same
night), I was "setup" to face yet
a second related encounter. (This time, alone!)

For nearly thirty, very long, drawn-out
minutes, I was hit with an on and off
series of "sweat-attacks!"
Perhaps, designed, to be some sort of
a cleaning process? (I'll leave
that small matter up to you!)

At any rate, the bottom bed sheet,
felt as though, I was lying in a
"pool of water." (Like a sprung,
water-bed leak!)
Only, it was my own sweat. Enough, to
even be seen and felt, on the
wooden floor-boards, directly
below. Making any walking, in
that area, very dangerous
because it was not only wet,
but also "very greasy!"

By washing the wet bed sheet and
putting it through several rigorous
twists and turns, it was nearly
dry by daybreak, And, the floor, had
become dry enough to safely walk
on. After using "several" tissue
paper swipes.

A warm, steady southerly breeze
continued to blow through the three
second-story opened windows.
Helping, to greet and welcome,
a brand new day. And, a chance
"to reflect," on a more positive
and stable future, to follow!

Reflect A

When will people (humans),
of "all ages" learn the
value of listening,
sharing and working
side-by-side, together?!
(Reflect, for the day.)

Visions (The Physical Kind)

Visions, are "very common,"
among the general public,
at-large.
Or so, I have read.

Anytime, a physically seen
object (alive, dead or otherwise),
changes its shape or its looks,
it can be clearly called,
"a vision!"

In my own lifetime,
(as of 04-04-13),
the number of physical visions I've had,
total no more than 5.

Some individuals
regardless, of their place of birth,
cultural, ethnic, or social backgrounds,
or even their chronological ages,
may have had more than 5, less
than 5, or none at all!

Do "visions" talk?
I don't think so. (There might be exceptions.)
Are they "scary?"
No!
Surprising?
Always!

Visions, are able "to insist" upon,
your complete attention!
They also manage,
to bring people to a complete stop.
Whenever, they are seen.

Do visions have any "real" value
or "merit?"
My readings, about "this topic,"
are not very complete, nor that openly
detailed.
Based, upon my own personal experiences,
I think, they could!

Visions, I have found,
manage to make themselves known . . .
     1.   When, not invited.
     2.   When, not expected.
     3.   When, not wished for.
In summary, visions (the kind I'm writing
     about),
appear to be very independent spirits.

My first known vision (12-1997),
took place at an elementary school.
Just before leaving, at the end,
of a normal teaching day.

I remember, being stopped in the
main East-Area Hallway,
by an unusually shiny white

light, coming out from the opened
door belonging to the school nurse's
station.

A light, that had passed through a
small security window, separating
the nurse's work area from the
front office, at that time.

The window, itself, had now become
"much larger," so that it was possible,
to see those working on the other side.

The front office's background wall
was completely restricted,
by a low blanket of ground fog,
that was quickly being replaced with
a clean, plain hanging white sheet.
This, in turn, was rapidly
transformed into a sparkling beaded
curtain, that also turned into a
fast-flowing stream of river water,
that was rushing over a steeply cut
cliff, facing east.

Thus, creating a thunderous looking spray
that changed
into a light, puffy, cream-colored
mist.
A mist, that rose halfway up inside the
same busy front office wall. Thus, caused

(most likely) by "the unseen" bedrock, at the
base of the waterfall.

Meanwhile, the busy office workers
continued their individually assigned
duties.
Seemingly, unaware of what was really
happening,
just a few steps,
in back of them!

Then, just as unexpectedly,
the complete picture,
started "to fade" out-of-sight.
The "security window" returned
to its normal size, once again.

To the tune of many rushing
feet and many voices, the
building continued to empty as "the flow"
headed toward the waiting buses
and family cars, outside.

Strange! I was never asked,
"What are you doing?" (While standing in
the hallway).

Challenges

It had been, just about,
two weeks hence, when
I had my very first sighted-vision,
at a nearby elementary school.
(December 1977), that I received
my second encounter.

But, this one took place at home,
in the family kitchen, late one
Sunday afternoon.
My mother (Harriett), had been
having trouble keeping her
balance when either walking or
standing in one spot.

Now, while in our downstairs
bathroom, she also appeared to be
greatly confused and disoriented.
So, Joyce (sister), Kenneth (brother)
and I decided to call the
Brentwood Ambulance for
some help.

Once, they promptly arrived,
our mother was carefully
placed on their stretcher and
securely strapped-down.

Before, the attendants could
quickly leave, there were
some "last minute" sign off
papers that needed to be taken care of and
approved.

In the meantime, Mum and I
were waiting between the wood-electric
combination
stove and the clothes dryer, to the east.

I was standing at the foot
of the stretcher, between the
two listed objects.
Suddenly, without any warning,
Mum started to slowly move her
head from side to side.
Was she in more pain? Was she
looking for a kitchen fixture?
Was she looking for someone
to talk to?

My questions, or at least one of
them, were about to be answered.
Because several things started to
happen, all at once!
Mum was undergoing a major
physical transformation, while still in her pj's.

Mum's body length
had increased to six feet,
from her standard 5'3" height.

Her hairstyle became
very different, allowing for
her now "new" fully healthy (no white)
crop, to flow easily across
her high forehead in a most
graceful and free
like manner. (Even with
her glasses and while still
strapped in.)

Skin texture:
No, wrinkles.
No, brown age spots.
No, Magnusson skin blemishes.
Someone, between their late
30s to early 40s in perfect
physical shape!

New set of clothes:
A one-piece, summer designed,
casual skirt,
High neckline,
Covered, kneecaps.
Style? Yellow background, several scattered
large green-lined blocks with thin scrolls,
mixed in. Attractive!

Shoes and dress stockings:
Mum also "sported"
a pair of dark, spiked high
dress shoes and a pair of
long dress stockings, to
match.

All together, "the changes" pointed and
projected a person full of
"renewed" youthfulness, life, energy and
positive determination!

Now, my mother started to
focus her sights toward me.
Giving me, one of her "well-known"
unblinking, forcefully directed
brown-eyed looks!

The kind, whenever there was
a job to be started, corrected or
to be finished.
Those two eyes "always" expected
to see some movement, forthwith!

In this particular instance,
both pupils also started to slowly
grow larger and larger. (Up to the same
size of a standard golf ball, used
on a fairway.)
All before I was able to manage
to insert a quietly whispered,
"Hi, Mum!"

Even though my response time
was "exceedingly" slow, it still was
very quickly acknowledged.
Her physical appearance and
the visual sightings of the
immediate surroundings,
slowly began "to retrack" to
their normal beginnings.

During this rather unexpected
turn of events, no one from
the west side of the kitchen,
had looked "our way" or had
seemingly realized that there
had also been a second story
taking place (within easy sight
and normal sound levels), that
fateful, late afternoon.

A Near-Death Surprise!

The Prelude
It was a beautiful,
early, summerlike,
mid-June (2004) day.
My watch said that it
was time "to get back,
to work!"

The weather was perfect
for mowing home lawns, that day!
It was sunny, with a good, warm
drying breeze.
Someone might even have
ventured to add that it was
a perfect afternoon to do some
"fly-fishing."

Unfortunately, our back field
pond (once used to irrigate
our potato fields), now stays
dormant.
It depends only on snow and
rain "run-offs," to be kept full,
most of the time.

No springs.
Only limited water life exists.
Not the best spot for creatures
needing a steady flow of fresh
water, over a long period of
time. And food, missing!

Any, frogs? Yes.
Any, turtles? Sometimes.
Any, weedy-weeds? Always.
Any, fish to eat? No.
Any, muddy pond bottoms? Most of it.
Any, "Cat-o'-Nine tails?" Always.
Any, teeny tiny fishes? No.

Suddenly, my front steering
tires got stuck!
Both wheels were caught
in a deep "V" shaped rut,
located at the southwestern (compass
location)
end of the standing-pond.

So, I was officially blocked!
I looked around.
Then, shifted into reverse
"rather quickly,"
to get freed and to be able
to continue my grass cuttings.

Well! I got "cleared" alright!
Only to find myself
completely airborne!
Thus, stretched out
straight (feet, facing south),
with lots of free space
all around me!

For what seemed like about six
lengthy eye blinks,
I unexpectedly found out
just how it felt,
to be completely free
from the forces-of-gravity,
with nothing to touch
or to hang on to.
(Words cannot tell, what it
was really like.)
Pretty amazing stuff! Believe!

The Drama
Just as quickly, I next
found myself
in a crouched position,
facing north,
much like that of a
baseball catcher,
at home plate.
(only, this time, in water)
with nothing to see or look at,
up ahead.

At the same time,
I felt,
a large flat rectangular
object of "smooth metal"
or so I first thought,
resting on my head and back.
About 3–4 inches thick, based

on what my fingers felt.
Not that heavy at the time,
I suppose,
because the two of us were
covered over with the same pond water depth.

My first, suggested "thought wave."
"Need to get off, to move!"
I did as I was told.
Which, sounded like a logical
suggestion, not a command or a
required order.

By reaching upward, I felt
a metal bar (the cutting blade)
and the carriage-rim,
underneath.
Then, I started to push the
lawn mower (right) to get
it out of the way and off of me.
(There was some "dead-weight." Expected.)
Slow to push. And, slow to move.
Still, I saw no waterline ahead or
around me.

Instead, there was a large, tall thin,
upright, wood-grained,
rectangular window frame facing me,
like those often seen in the old elementary
one-room schools.
The top half of the glass plate

was a yellowish, spotted brown.
The bottom half, of similar size glass,
was a light gray color.

My second suggested "thought-wave,"
advised me to always remember
The Window! No reason, except to take
note. (Very strongly and clearly
mentioned, only once!!)

Okay! So how was I to do that?
A list of ideas rushed through
my head.

1.) If I had a camera, I could
    take a picture.

2.) If I had a box of colored-
    crayons, I could try to
    reproduce what "my eyes" saw.

3.) If I had just a pencil and
    a piece of plain drawing
    paper, I could make a
    black and white outline.

4.) If I had an art brush
    with a set of colored tube
    samples to spread on a textured
    cloth frame, that . . .
    might also work.

5.) If I had a tape recorder,
    a voice-given picture, could
    be made.

But, since I had none of
the above, I figured, that
my senior-ageless gray cells
would have to step forward,
and do their very best.

Only by looking "carefully" through
the window-frame, was
there any clue of a possible
waterline. (I wouldn't have
dared gamble, one way or the other.)

By now, at this juncture, I
started to realize, how very
quiet and peaceful I felt!
Even with, both eyes and mouth
open, I didn't feel any inward
or outward "personal stress." Wonderful!

I remember thinking, if only
the water temperature was
just "a pinch" warmer!
How very easily, I could thus
close my eyes and drop off
into a deep sleep.

But, you see, that never happened
because the temperature of
the water never reached, that special
"next-step."

Of course, if it had,
Then there would be no
"near-death" experience, to
write about.
Right? . . . Right!

My third suggested "thought-wave":
"Need to get some air."
So, I started heading toward
the water's surface.
Once, I had broken above
"the mysterious" waterline,
I had no trouble, continuing . . .
At full-speed-ahead!

Spitting out the pond water,
In my mouth . . .
while en route.

No, water held up in my nose!
No, urgent need to gulp in
tons of "fresh air."
No, sore eyes (total time
estimated under water,
nearly ten minutes).

No, coughing, from a prolonged
lack-of-air either.
No, upset stomach, having eaten (a hearty)
noon meal, just thirty
minutes before.

My fourth, suggested "thought-wave":
"Need to see if you can move."
So, folks, there I was moving
my head, arms, fingers, ears.
Yes, even, my toes!
Nothing appeared broken or
not functioning.

That "testing" suggestion, carried out,
must have been quite a
sight!
Half in and half out
of the water.

I was also covered from head-
to-toe with pond mud,
grasses, weeds and other
junk, I don't remember.

The Summary
I. There were no eyewitnesses, at the time
    of the accident.

2. The John Deere STX-30 is built with a safety switch designed to "shut off" the engine, once any driver leaves the front seat while the mower is in the "driving position."

3. My whole left half side was sore for a number of days, but no black and blue marks.

4. The lawnmower was found resting on its left side, when it was chain pulled from the water with the help of our next door neighbor's pick-up truck, Mr. Woodman, of Windy Hill Farm.

5. My brother Bob (a certified machine mechanic) checked out the engine, later that same afternoon. It was water logged! Still, the lawnmower started up, after drainage. Sounding great, despite its pond water bath.

6. My sister Joyce had gone walking during the time "the accident" took place. By the time she'd returned, I'd managed to take a bath and changed into clean clothes.

7. It's taken a long time, just to grasp how very lucky I really was.

8. During the beginning stages of the accident, there were a number of "blank spots" that I still cannot account for. A mild concussion? Maybe. At the time, it seemed as though, I was getting a lot of mental support from an area located just above the right-ear. A somewhat triangular feeling spot that projected itself toward the back of my head in the shape of an arrowhead. Thus, being able to take over "all necessary" bodily functions that had been "shut down" or maybe even detoured, very probably! There was a small void, like an unfeeling empty spot, that remained for a number of days just above the right-ear area, which later, formed an oval-like sphere before disappearing all together. Thankfully, my eyesight was never affected.

JODY A. LONG
Attorney at Law

Jody A. Long, PLLC
535 Dock St., Suite 108
Tacoma, WA 98402
Telephone: (253) 572-1330
Facsimile: (253)572-1344

October 19, 2004

Sid Gove
119 South Rd.
Brentwood, NH 03833-6300

RE: Experience

Dear Sid,

I want to thank you for submitting to the website. You do have a fascinating experience. I want to apologize for not getting back to you sooner. It is a bit difficult to maintain 3 websites and work 50 hours per week.

I am not sure what actually happened to you. There are categories of experiences that fall under the "other" category on www.oberf.org. I have continually reminded people that it really isn't about the "classification" of the experience, but rather how one reacts to it and how they integrate it into their daily lives. I think you had an event of spirit. That should help you integrate into your daily life that there is more to the body than your earthly mind. For example, if I had your experience, I'd be thinking along the lines of the immortal soul. I hope that answers your question. Please feel free to read the experiences on all 3 websites. They will also add to you knowledge and understanding of what constitutes and earthly experience and what constitutes one from spiritual origin.

Again, thank you for your patience.

Sincerely,

Jody A. Long

Jody A. Long, Webmaster
www.nderf.org
www.oberf.org
www.aderf.org

Letter in response to Sid Gove's account of a possible NDE from Jody A. Long who, along with her husband Dr. Jeff Long, runs the Near Death Experience Research Foundation (NDERF), an organization and website that researches NDEs and investigates how unconscious people can form conscious memories.

Reflect B

Now that I've reached "80,"
looking back,
how did I ever manage to pass "30?"
(Reflect for the day.)

A Sleep Vision/Cut Short

On the evening of December 4, 2004,
I experienced a "sleep vision" event. I'd never
read that such a thing could ever happen, but I
believe it did this time.

The Event
I was sitting outside,
by our front driveway,
with my back against the house wall,
next to the kitchen,
on the other side.

I was thoughtfully,
looking up at the puffy white clouds,
drifting on by,
in a northward direction.

Suddenly, a patch of puffy white
clouds started to change their
color and regrouped into a darkened
mass, just above me.
Was it about to rain?
The weather reports never mentioned it.
This was expected to be just another
pleasant spring-like morning.

To my further astonishment,
located in the upper-left corner
of this gathering glob,
appeared a small white stone-cut
base,

that continued to grow larger in size,
as each second ticked by.
A triangular platform, able to support
the unknown woman on top wearing a
formal dressing gown.

The "object-of-interest" was
from a solid piece of smooth, dark-
colored metal, with a wide floor-length
flowing skirt, commonly pictured in
Mrs. Lincoln's day.

As the statue slowly continued
downward, I wondered, just who
it might be?

1.) Someone, of military service
    and rank?
2.) Someone, with a public or private
    company?
3.) Someone, over-looked by past
    history, until now?

But, my thoughts were being broken
apart by the "ongoing foggy mists,"
swilling about this unknown figure,
that was wearing a hooded cap,
concealing her face.
Seemingly, "intended" to protect her
identity, until the proper moment
had arrived.

Circling, just above her head,
was a set of 12–14 unattached extra
small white-coated light bulbs. Each
focused, only, upon this exceptionally
tall and stately figure, as she
slowly drifted earthward, in front
of me.

But, sadly, here comes "the punch-
line!" At just about this point in her
descent, I thought,
"Oh! No! Not again!"
(Thinking of a similar visual picture
occurrence, in June of 2004).

That seemingly very innocently
projected thought, caused this
on-going powerful picture drama
to vanish before me!
Only to be replaced by the puffy
white clouds, that once again,
were traveling north.

Aftermath
I submit, that the sighted
image, of the unknown
woman placed upon the moving
triangular (3-sided) platform
should not be quickly forgotten
nor over-looked.

One might be tempted to seriously contemplate, quite honestly, that what I saw (briefly) was "the shadow" of one of the three known goddesses of classical mythology, who determines the course of human life.

A Quick, Flyby Visit

Visions are, indeed, very unpredictable
and very mysterious. But, as far
as I know, they are not dangerous!

On January-2011, I was called
to our downstairs bathroom, due to
stomach cramps.

As I passed through the open
bathroom door, I felt that I
might be a part of another
"window event."

Because there, floating in the
cleanly-settled wastewater's
toilet bowl, was a floating U.S.
Postcard, with a black and white head
profile in the center, of my
late father (Herbert), looking eastward
toward the Atlantic Ocean? Or,
maybe, across toward England!

He appeared to be in his late 30s
to early 40s. Crew cut. White hair.
Wearing a casual (open neck) sports shirt.
Appeared rested and relaxed.
And, with a closed mouth smile
on his face, so often seen.

But, before I could reach to pick
up the floating postcard, his
picture and the card both quickly disappeared.

Appendix: *The Gove Book*

Shortly, before I selected a publisher to print 30 copies of *A Time to Sing!* I wrote to Gove, Kansas (made known to me, by Stan Gove and his wife Elaine, who had once visited.)

Ms. Marcia Roemer, Curator of the Gove County Museum, provided me with some general and specific facts about Gove, Kansas and *The Gove Book* - 1922.

First, the "original" editions of *The Gove Book* - 1922, are no longer publicly available! Those that do exist have become collector items, running upwards to $1,500.00 or even higher based on their present-condition. (I happen to own an "original" edition, sold to me while in high school by my Uncle John Gove, with its deep-rose colored hard covers and yellow-tinted letterings.)

Today, that same book has weathered some "rough-years" and has lost much of its "physical" value.

However, "copies" (thereof) can still be ordered by contacting www.amazon.com, for about $50.00 (more or less).

Secondly, Gove, Kansas is a lightly-settled hard-working rural community, that is just barely holding its own.

Hopefully, someone reading this account, with the education, time and management skills will form a long-term "study-plan," including financial support and a carefully directed-script, that would be able to work.

Attn. Ms. Marcia Roemer
Curator
Gove County Museum
Gove, Kansas   67736
Phone (785) 938-2385
E-mail: roemer_dm@hotmail.com

About the Author

Born July 2, 1931, Exeter, NH
Lifelong resident of Brentwood, NH
Exeter (Tuck) High School, 1950
US Navy/Korean War, 1951–54
Keene State College, 1960 B. Ed.
Gorham State College, 1968 M.S. Ed.
University of Southern Maine, 1973 M.S. Ed.
Classroom Teacher/Elementary (R)
Started writing soon after 09-11-01

Other Publications:

From Me to You! (2008) Vantage Press
'Til, We Meet Again! (2011) Vantage Press

www.ingramcontent.com/pod-product-compliance
Lightning Source LLC
LaVergne TN
LVHW051850080426
835512LV00018B/3171